DON'T RETIRE RE-FIRE

SHEILA WHITE

Order this book online at www.trafford.com
or email orders@trafford.com

Most Trafford titles are also available at major online book retailers.

© Copyright 2023 Sheila White.

All rights reserved. No part of this publication may be reproduced, stored in a retrieval system, or transmitted, in any form or by any means, electronic, mechanical, photocopying, recording, or otherwise, without the written prior permission of the author.

Print information available on the last page.

ISBN: 978-1-6987-1555-1 (sc)
ISBN: 978-1-6987-1556-8 (e)

Library of Congress Control Number: 2023919137

Because of the dynamic nature of the Internet, any web addresses or links contained in this book may have changed since publication and may no longer be valid. The views expressed in this work are solely those of the author and do not necessarily reflect the views of the publisher, and the publisher hereby disclaims any responsibility for them.

Any people depicted in stock imagery provided by Getty Images are models, and such images are being used for illustrative purposes only.
Certain stock imagery © Getty Images.

All scripture quotes are from the King James Version of the Holy Bible.

Trafford rev. 11/06/2023

 www.trafford.com

North America & international
toll-free: 844-688-6899 (USA & Canada)
fax: 812 355 4082

DON'T RETIRE RE-FIRE
Rediscovering Yourself In Your Later Years

Presented to: _____

From Author: _____

Date: _____

CONTENTS

Dedication ix
Acknowledgements xi
Introduction xiii

Chapter 1 Retire Or Re-Fire 1
Chapter 2 Too Legit To Quit 11
Chapter 3 Rediscover Yourself 20
Chapter 4 It's Never Too Late 26
Chapter 5 Deal With The Root Not The Fruit 34
Chapter 6 What Do You Make Of Your Sage? 44
Chapter 7 Opportunity Or Crisis 51

Epilogue 59
About The Author 61

DEDICATION

I dedicate this book to my Lord and Savior, Jesus Christ, for helping me understand that my gifts do not retire and my talents are for the glory of God throughout my lifetime. To the memory of my father and mother, Gene McDaniel and Lorraine Bunton.

I also dedicate this book to Glen White, my loving husband, who has supported me throughout this project. To my three angels here on earth, Michael, David, and Gabrielle White, you three are my reasons for refiring my life. To my niece Christina and my Road 2 Eternity Media team and Skyward Books crew. You guys rock!

Also, my siblings, Joyce, William, Sandra, Betty, Eugene, Wayne, Darnell, Gloria, and Rose. Who keep refiring their lives.

And to my best friend, Irene Youngblood, for your friendship and support throughout the years.

ACKNOWLEDGEMENTS

I want to give a special thank you to our team at Skyward Books, Michael White, for bringing the fantastic cover design into reality. In addition, I want to shine the light on Gabrielle White for your incredible photography. I also want to thank Diana K. Bell, who has supported me throughout this project.

Also, I want to thank my good friends, Michael Bart and Robbie Mathews, who are part of our Skyward Books family, and our mentors and coaches.

INTRODUCTION

The traditional old-school definition of retirement is to leave one's job or cease working, typically upon retirement age. Dependent upon your traditional retirement age, if you work 40-hours per week for 40-years of your life, you will be eligible to retire on 40 percent of your income around the age of 66 or 67, even older, depending on what year you were born.

A non-traditional way of thinking about retirement: Retirement is not based on age. Retirement is based on income. So, ask yourself this question: If at the exact age you are today, if you had enough income to cover your outflow, month after month, would you keep on working every day?

This book will help you embrace a fresh viewpoint about retirement. You can refine your ambitions and set your sails towards new goals. You can decide how you will continue to grow at this stage of your life.

As stated earlier, retirement is not about age; it is not about a number, meaning a person can stop working at age 40 because they have enough financial security to maintain their lifestyle for the remainder of their lives.

They may choose to fulfill other goals in life while helping others to do the same. Retirement is not so much about how old you are but about the decisions you make along the way that will enable you to achieve the financial success needed to retire, regardless of your age. It does not matter whether you have one job or many career choices. We all should think about the next stage in our life after our working years as an employee are over.

We will address the refiring part later in this book. First, however, looking back on our lives, we will better understand the major themes and influences that guided us. Do not entrust the final say of your future to a dysfunctional (financial or otherwise) group of people who cannot even function without dysfunction.

It is essential and can be liberating to reflect deeply on what you want for your own life that has yet to come. Socrates said: "An unexamined life is not worth living."

This book will empower you to examine your past and present life and take you on a journey to refine your life after retirement from a job or career. You will read about dreams, visions, and how to dust off your goals. Your transformation will enable you to think, feel, and act within the paradigm of your own choices. While you may have thought retirement was the endgame, you now hold in your hands a roadmap, with several spiritual guideposts to assist you along your journey.

It is my sincere desire for you to re-fire your life within the pages of this book. Happy reading!!!

CHAPTER ONE

RETIRE OR RE-FIRE

A lot of adults have jobs or careers that they do not particularly enjoy. Many people make lots of money on their jobs, but they do not fully realize their dreams. Here is a question to ask yourself: Are you moving at a pace in your work and personal life that optimizes your full potential?

Some people may feel they do not have the support, resources, money, or knowledge to do things differently. That is why millions of people act like robots every morning after waking up. That group only knows one thing – home-to-work-work-to-home, day in and day out, same routine.

The fact that you are reading this book means you are taking steps towards transforming your life! You made a significant step, so let's keep going. You have it in you to map out and discover your next career, your next relationship, your next health plan, and your next view on life.

Our imagination is an incredible force that can create new paths and turn the once 'thought impossible' into 'possible' achievements. Finding your Re-fire moment of clarity as you get older, knowing your purpose, working on your passion, and, more importantly, understanding that making an impact in this world can be a game-changer.

Fire up your faith, not your fears. Retirement age is not the time to give up on making new goals or stop dreaming. My daughter

(Gabrielle) says: "When relying on societies stereotypes to be your standard, telling you who you are, who you are going to be, and all you will ever become, you miss the mark and reality of the totality of your potential, purpose, and stone written promises of God for yourself."

C.S. Lewis says: "You are never too old to start another goal or another dream." Continue to read, learn, grow, and sharpen your iron. (Proverbs 27:17), says: "Iron sharpens iron; so a man sharpens the countenance of his friend." Align yourself with principles that will help you excel and keep on keeping on.

SHEILA'S SPARKS: When You Discover Your Uniqueness, You Are Bonded With Jesus.

The power of believing in your abilities at your current age will empower you to show up and be deliberate towards achieving your goals. I can relate the power of believing in your abilities to the iron sharpens iron principle. I have aligned myself (over the years) with like-minded people who empower me to reach goals that I thought I never could achieve.

Three examples of me reaching some of my transformational goals include #1. I started my podcast (Gifted With Sheila White). #2. Going into the film and television industry (Road 2 Eternity Media). #3. Becoming a published author of two books (Discover Your Uniqueness & Don't Retire Re-fire). I am refiring my goals and dreams and not settling for less.

SHEILA'S SPARKS: When The Dream Is Big Enough, The Facts Do Not Count.

The more I develop a closer relationship with God, which I believe is a key to refiring, the more I see that He is faithful and will not leave me nor forsake me.

Part of my ongoing developing relationship with God also comes from scriptures written in the excellent book. As you read on, take copious Re-fire notes that resonate with where you are today in life. Then, using the new paradigm of thought; Don't Retire Re-fire. Pay special attention to what that looks like for you. Then begin right where you are to start your transformational journey.

Throughout my earthly journey, I have experienced setbacks, roadblocks, speed bumps, even failures over the test of time. However, God never left me, and I never gave up my faith in God. I believe that God wanted me to be a better person for myself, more than I wanted for myself.

(Jeremiah 29:11) "For I know the plans I have for you declares the Lord, plans to prosper and not to harm you, plans to give you hope and a future." Also, (Matthew 28:20) says: "Lo I am with you always, even unto the end of the world."

Even when we stumble and fall in life or simply stop working in our retirement years, God is there to keep us encouraged, pick us up, and help us attain a new focus. (Psalm 46:1) says: "God is a present help in times of trouble."

Life after retirement can be exciting and empowering for some but empty and isolating for others. Retirement for some can be an extended vacation. If you do not have plans after retirement from your job or career, you may feel lonely, triggering other negative thoughts and emotions.

<u>SHEILA'S SPARKS</u> – Seek And Plan For Your Retirement Early In Your Career.

It is never too late. Begin right where you are today by making and committing to a solid financial refire, retirement plan of action.

Decades of the routine of keeping schedules give some people a sense of usefulness. The psychological frontier of retirement means something different to different people. Some people try to stay busy during this time that they work harder and are busier. That does not mean they are working on their dreams or goals; they are just busy.

Eventually, they must navigate their time and produce a plan if they don't want to burn out or get bored with being a volunteer in other people's activities. Good things are waiting for you, even though you might not have started planning before you retired.

(Romans 8:28) says: "And we know that all things work together for the good to those who love God, and to those who are called according to His purpose." Realizing that the work-life has ceased (retirement), and you have been looking for this moment for so many years, now that you have retired, it seems like it is not what retirement is supposed to be. Do not believe the hype!!!

You can still enjoy your newfound liberty. Do not feel guilty about saying no just because you have the time on your hands. God still has a plan for your life regardless of your age. Prayer is a way to seek and know God's plan for your life. Take the time to meditate on God's word in the bible.

(Jeremiah 29:13) says: "And ye shall seek me and find me when ye shall search for me with all your heart." You still have value. Do not let retirement paralyze what you can still offer the world. (2 Timothy 1:7) says: "For God hath not given us a spirit of fear, but of power, love, and of a sound mind." God has told us in His word over and over again not to be afraid. (Psalm 46:1) says: "God is our refuge and strength, a very present help in trouble." We do not have to be afraid. Not afraid of retirement, not fearful of refiring our lives. God is our bridge over troubled waters.

SHEILA'S SPARKS: Planning To Re-Fire Your Life Before Retirement Will Provide You Better Opportunities To Enjoy The Fruits Of Your Labor During Retirement.

There may be fears about retirement when you have not planned for it. (Joshua 1:9) says: For the Lord, thy God will be with thee wherever thou goest." (Proverbs 3:5,6) says: "Trust in the Lord with all thine heart and lean not unto thine own understanding. In all thy ways acknowledge Him, and He shall direct thy paths."

Our world is full of many challenges. But God is still our refuge and strength. He is present when we need help in times of trouble. Our responsibility is to take action after asking for God's blessings and guidance over what we seek. Our society may look down on our senior citizens. Yet, there is a plethora of knowledge and wisdom within our senior citizen community for those who seek understanding.

The real wisdom and treasure are in our senior citizens because they have walked through the mind-fields of life and reached retirement. But, on the other hand, some young people stop dreaming and do not strive to achieve their goals.

Many young people do not seek the wise experience and advice from our many gifted retired seniors, that with wise counsel, can help young people not to step on as many land minds walking through their journey in life.

Les Brown – "It has been said, most people die at age twenty-five, and don't get buried until they are sixty-five. Try to live your life to the fullest." When young people step on a land mine (stop dreaming), they die mentally, yet they live on and do not get buried until old age. Their dreams died in their youth.

You do not have to experience a middle-aged crisis. You can hit the reset/Re-Fire button and try to live your best life. It is an individual's positive mental attitude and mindset that is the key to this transformation. That is the catalyst for achieving 'that retirement good life' that you desire to enjoy.

The reality of not hitting the reset/Re-Fire button is like having a midlife crisis. Experiencing a midlife crisis can be devastating. A person can become depressed and resentful to these close to them. They can become easily angered or rejected by those who love them because they do not feel good enough.

During this time, they may be suffering from imperfections from their past mistakes of not planning to Re-fire after Retirement. Good news – God loves imperfect people, and God does not turn away from you. The bible is full of imperfect people doing God's will.

Here is a shortlist of imperfect people like Noah, who was a drunk. Abraham lied about his wife, Sarah. Isaac was a daydreamer. Jacob was a liar, and Leah was ugly. His brothers abused Joseph, Moses had a stuttering problem, Gideon was afraid, and Samson was a womanizer.

Rahab was a prostitute, David was an adulterer, and Elijah was suicidal. Jonah ran away. Job who went bankrupt. John, who ate bugs. Peter denied Christ and Martha were worriers. The Samaritan woman was divorced multiple times. Zacchaeus, who was small, and Lazarus, who was dead. God used them as examples for goodwill.

Use what you have in your season of life to be an effective change-maker in this world.

Les Brown says: "You Have Greatness In You." Serve others, be a faithful steward over what God's grace has in various forms of your life. God does not call the equipped; he equips the called. It is not about your ability at this age; it's about your availability.

<u>SHEILA'S SPARKS:</u> By Finding Your Moment Of Spiritual Clarity, You Can Discover Your Power Within."

(Philippians 4:13) says: "I can do all things through Christ who strengthens me." Your talents and gifts are still inside of you. The gifts that God instilled inside of us do not retire. You were born with greatness. Good things can happen even when we go through dark places in our lives. Babies develop inside the darkness of a mother's womb.

God spoke to the darkness and said, let there be light. The Shepherds were watching their flocks in the dark of night. But they were guided by the stars and light from the moon, so do not stop. Keep your light shining bright; keep climbing until you reach the mountain top of achievement. Keep dreaming big dreams, keep working on your goals. Maintain your focus, refine, and re-fire the desires that you want to accomplish. You are abiding under the shadow of the light from the almighty.

The Lord is your refuge and strength. In Him, you can trust. Listen to that internal voice that awakens your soul. That same voice of reason can guide you in life. God's call on our lives is not a one-size voice that fits all. Instead, God has used people of all ages and different professions to bring transformation and change into this world.

There is no young or old age limitation for service in the kingdom of God. An old saying, 'You can take the dog out of the fight, but you can't take the fight out of the dog.' But, there is a light at the end of the tunnel. Learn to have fun, make new friends, maintain social contacts, stay physically active, and consider part-time work or volunteering. The most important thing to remember is what you have to offer this world at any age is your assignment from God.

Pay attention to your legacy. What is a legacy? Miriam Webster's definition of legacy – "A gift by (WILL) especially of money or personal property." A family or business legacy from parents to children and grandchildren) one generation to the next.

<u>SHEILA'S SPARKS:</u> Your Legacy Is What You Make It – Be Intentional!!!

Your Surname or family name is the history of your family legacy. Do you know anything about the following Surname? – Obama, Hilton, Winfrey, Vanderbilt, Rockefeller, Forbes, Ford, Rolls, Royce, Buffett, and Gates. We remember those names and countless others because of their legacy. (Luke 12:48) says: "To whom much is given, much will be required." When we are blessed with extraordinary talents, wealth, and knowledge, the art of blessing others should automatically become an easy decision.

The storyline of retirement and leaving a legacy should not be about the pot of gold at the end of the rainbow. Instead, your intentional legacy should be more about transforming oneself into the arena of who you help and who you serve. Do not allow this brief time in your earthly life to make you feel trapped or lose your sense of identity of who you are. You are more than just a retired teacher, professor, lawyer, performer, bus operator, athlete, or engineer. You are still someone special, with your unique God-given gifts.

Mentoring, coaching, and volunteering can lay the groundwork for having a fulfilling life after and during retirement. Even starting a new hobby on weekends can lead to a new transformation.

God did not create us for retirement. His original plan for humanity was everlasting life on earth. Adam and Eve messed up that plan with sin. However, God invented man, like a man invented an engine. Cars are designed to run on petrol and, or electricity. It would not run properly on anything else.

God designed the human machine to run on certain principles as well. God is the heavenly fuel and electricity that runs our mortal engines. Our spirits were designed to feed on Him. There is no other fuel or electricity here on earth that can match the high-octane fuel and electricity from God.

Trying to fill a void in our lives with money, alcohol, power, drugs, or materialism will not lead to fulfillment or a properly running human machine. Instead, a life in Christ can provide a roadmap, guidepost, and compass to help guide the direction of your life.

Retirement does not always go as planned, as many may know. However, retirement can drastically change your entire life depending on making a good solid financial retirement plan. Retirement is a refiring adjustment time for the next chapter in your life. Retiring your life is about understanding that the never-ending universe has filled the earth with all the resources needed for humanity, not just to survive but to re-fire and thrive at any age.

SHEILA'S SPARKS: If You Choose To Accept It, Your Mission Is To Find Your Purpose And Share It With The World.

Even if you are a late bloomer, share your purpose so that others can benefit from your life. You are at the top of God's creation, created in His image after His likeness.

Dr. James Dentley says: "When you change the way you look at things, the things you look at will change." Earl Nightingale says: "We become what we think about." Speak about the life you want to live and that special something that you desire most in life to achieve. It is not the number of years of life; it is the value of your life that counts (your legacy).

Refine your dreams, start a new list of goals. (Matthew 7:7) says: "Ask, and it shall be given you, seek and ye shall find; knock, and it shall be opened unto you." You might have started out living a mediocre life, then worked 50 or 60 years, creating an ordinary life. However, with God's help, you can strategically plan and Re-fire your life to live an extraordinary life.

In your later years, sometimes the chatter of noise and busyness in other areas of your life drowns out God's voice when he is speaking to us.

Here is a short story. In the bible, David was a young man who delighted to follow God. However, later in David's life, he lost his intimacy with God, which led him to sin. His actions nearly caused David to lose his kingdom.

As an older man, David became wiser in thought and weaker in the body. Finally, he realized he needed to return to God. In (Matthew 11:28,29) Jesus said: "Come unto Me all ye that are heavily laden, and I will give you rest, take my yoke upon you, and learn of Me for I am meek and lowly in heart, and ye shall find rest unto your soul." End of Story.

Do not let your decisions or choices hold you back from moving forward. People do not plan to fail; they fail to plan. By taking little or no action towards your retirement future, other than an exit date, you conform to a plan that might not serve you in your elder years.

Dream, plan and believe again. Fire up your imagination (Habakkuk 2:2) says: "And the Lord answered me and said, Write the vision, and make it plain upon the tables that he may run that readeth it." Your present-day tablet is your word document or your composition book. In other words, write down your vision and make it plain.

Having goals and working towards achieving them is a form of refiring. It is ok to receive coaching at this stage in life to better your best. However, we still need S.M.A.R.T goals to empower the refiring process of our lives. There are countless benefits for those who use S.M.A.R.T. goals.

What are S.M.A.R.T. goals?

<u>S</u>pecific – Write down your goals. Identify who, besides yourself, is responsible for achieving said goals. <u>M</u>easurable – How many, how much, and how often must you indulge until you achieve your goals. <u>A</u>chievable – What is your fixed date of achievement attached to your goals? Do you have all the resources needed for achievement, and are the expected results realistic? <u>R</u>elevant – Will your dreams make a

difference in your personal life? In your business life and the lives of others? <u>T</u>imebound – Did you begin with the end in mind? Meaning, what results should you achieve along the way?

What are your thoughts about retirement because your thoughts matter? "What you think about you bring about." – Dr. Johnnie Coleman used to say. Good, bad, or indifferent, a dream without a plan is like having faith without works. (James 2:20) says: "But wilt thou know, O vain man, that faith without works is dead?" God does not want you to live a life of pain and struggle in your retirement years.

The bible says in (3 John 1:2), "Beloved, I wish above all things that thou may prosper and be in health, even as thy soul prosper." Refiring in life comes from doing rewarding, meaningful, purposeful things throughout your life.

SHEILA'S SPARKS: You Can Re-Fire Your Life By Harnessing The Power Of Purpose.

You can also stagnate your life by harnessing the negative power of your thoughts. You can struggle in life by allowing the negative influence of thought to rule your mind. Your mind, not your age, can help you feel powerful or powerless.

Decide that you will live a purpose-driven life throughout your senior years so that you can leave a positive contribution, known as your legacy, to society. You can redefine and rediscover yourself in your later years. You can bring joy and happiness into your golden years. Refiring your life is not something you find; it is something you do. Ruth Casey said: "It only takes one person to change your life, You!" So Don't Retire; Re-fire is about your endless potential in life. To raise your frequency, renew your energy, make the best of your time, boost your confidence, build better relationships, shape up your finances, and begin to feel inspired.

CHAPTER TWO

TOO LEGIT TO QUIT

Years ago, an artist named M.C. Hammer, an American rapper, dancer, entertainer, record producer, and entrepreneur, was famous. However, he had his most tremendous commercial success and popularity in the late 1980s and 1990s. One of his big hits was a song titled Too Legit to Quit.

Too legit to quit means: You do not have to retire and sit out of the game of life and merely exist. You can Re-fire your retirement by redefining your purpose and asking yourself this question; who can I help, who can I serve, mentor or coach? It means you are too legit to stop dreaming, growing, and contributing more to society.

Legit can be another meaning for being cool. So, too legit means you are too cool to stop. Legit, a shortened version of the word legitimate, means conforming to laws, rules, regulations, authority, or leadership. Most people buy into the original idea of retirement as a time to relax and kick back after working 40 or 50 years on a job.

You are unstoppable in your creativity and imagination; you are too legit not to quit. Now think a bit, you might have to sit for a while, but you are too legit to quit. There is something about giving up. It feels like something withers away inside of us. It seems like you must fight the urge to quit. Some people stop when things get tough. But, when the tough get going, they become too legit to quit.

SHEILA'S SPARKS: Believe And Keep The Faith.

The bible talks about fighting the good fight of faith. Always keep the faith. Even though you might lose friends, you might lose business deals, and you might lose your material possessions. Lean onto the eternal spiritual life. Live and finish the course by keeping the faith.

(Exodus 14:14) says: "The Lord will fight for you while you keep silent." Meaning; remain faithful to God and keep His word even in the face of opposition, oppression, and adversity. Because through every hardship, there is a seed of greatness.

It means having an unswerving allegiance to the cause of God against all hostilities in the church and the world. And by any means necessary, do not give up on God; keep the faith. He will not give up on you. Differentiate what you can change and what you cannot change.

Think of what else is possible before you lose faith, give in, and give up. Look for the lessons in every situation. Keep a positive mental attitude within your thought process. Focus on creating new skills that will bring you the necessary solution-based results that you seek because you kept the faith while finding your moment of clarity.

Spend time with people that support you. Ask for help sooner rather than later. Get a second opinion and find a creative outlet. You can harness the power of purpose by reading inspirational, motivational, personal development, and self-help materials.

It is time to take a breath of fresh air by going outdoors, get inspired, get re-fired, and take it all in to gain perspective. (Joshua 1:9) says: "Be strong and courageous, do not be frightened or dismayed, for the Lord, your God is with you wherever you go."

When your life has its ups, downs, struggles, or hardships that make you want to quit, remember you are not going at it alone.

SHEILA'S SPARKS: You Are Too Legit To Quit.

(Deuteronomy 31:6,8) says: "Be strong and bold, have no fear or dread of them because it is the Lord your God who goes before you. He will be with you. He will not fail you or forsake you." Having faith in God and trusting in His strength is the power to see us through.

(1 Peter 5:7) says: "Cast your cares on Him because He cares for you."

(Matthew 6:25-27) says: "Therefore I tell you do not be anxious about your life, what you shall eat, or what you will drink, nor about your body, what you will put on, is life, not more than food, and the body more than clothing? Look at the birds of the air, they neither sow nor reap nor gather into barns, yet your heavenly Father feeds them. Are you not of more value than they? And which of you, by being anxious, can add a single hour to his span of life?"

Also, (Psalm 121:1-2) says: "I will lift up my eyes to the hills, from where my help comes, my help comes from the Lord who made heaven and earth." Many scriptures tell us to be courageous, not give up, and keep the faith. (Proverbs 3:5) says: "With all your heart and trust in the Lord, lean not on your own understanding, in all your ways submit to Him, and He will make your paths straight." Benjamin Franklin said: "If you fail to plan, you plan to fail." Refine yourself, Re-fire your thoughts. Set new goals and work towards achieving them. Ralph Waldo Emerson said: "A man is what he thinks about, all day long." Napoleon Hill said: "Whatever the mind of man can conceive and believe, it can achieve."

God wants you to walk a meaningful purpose-driven journey your entire life. So, renew your faith, find your moment of clarity, harness your power of purpose, identify your chief aim in life, write down your action plan for achievement, and take action NOW!!!

We must defy the urge to quit. When you have experienced the taste of finishing/winning, it encourages you not to give up. There is something contagious about finishing/winning in the game of life, liberty, and the pursuit of happiness.

SHEILA'S SPARKS: Quitting Is Not An Option If You Want To Win In The Game Of Life.

When you experience pressing through the heartache and pain and continue to fight on, no matter the circumstances, you are a winner. It builds your resolve; it strengthens your 'I can do it' attitude. Regardless of what winners had to sacrifice along the way (friendships, time, and money), they still believed they could make it.

They were broke and lonely, but they still believed. People betrayed them, but they still believed. Many people have fought with liars, backstabbers, haters, and naysayers along their journey of achievement. On many occasions, those same people even fought with themselves within their minds and thoughts.

Coming from their own self-limiting beliefs within their mind, they began listening to self-sabotaging negativity. Their breakthrough moment of clarity came when they started to change their thinking. When you change your thinking, you change your feelings; when you change your feelings, you change your actions.

They did not mentally stay a wandering generality and let those thoughts take residence in their mind. They believe they could make it. They did not quit. They did not keep thinking the same thing and expect different results; they changed their thoughts.

You are not defeated by what other people think or say about you. The defeat comes when you believe what the wanna doers, gonna doers, naysayers, and never doers say about you. Then, they have no power over you unless you decide to admit defeat, wave the white flag, tap out, give up and quit.

Paul wrote to Timothy in the bible about fighting the good fight. (1 Timothy 6:12) "Fight the good fight of faith, lay hold on eternal life, whereunto thou art also called, and has professed a good profession before many witnesses. You can take the dog out of the fight, but you cannot take the fight out of the dog. There is a danger of living a life of incompleteness.

Finishers/winners do not have time to pay attention to other people's business because they focus on finishing/winning.

SHEILA'S SPARKS: It Does Not Matter If You Run Your Race Fast Like The Rabbit or Slow Like The Turtle. As Long As You Cross The Finish Line, You Are A Winner.

Jesus, in the garden of Gethsemane (Matthew 26:36-46), was tempted to quit, but He kept going. He prayed to God to help Him finish. Jesus finished His assignment. He said, not My will but Your will God, as He resisted the urge to cave in and quit.

This life here on earth is not Burger King! Meaning you do not get to have it your way. Stick it out until the end. Cross your finish line at your own pace. You may not look pretty or cross the finish line first. And you may not win a trophy. But when care is pressing you down a bit – pause if you must, but do not quit.

Before I go into the dream, let's shine some light on education for a moment.

Yes, I fully support education, and I admire those who took the traditional brick-and-mortar old school route who earned their degree. However, how many people are there with an associate, bachelor's, master's, even their Ph.D.? How many of those same people with degrees cannot find employment or must settle for a minimum wage job because of the issues that confront us today? We all know that it is hard to be successful.

Would you agree that achieving success is hard? If you do not believe me, ask the person (with the degree) who is earning minimum wage to survive.

However, the DREAM is the most important education that you can receive during your lifetime. The dream is your master key for success, not the how-to. When the aim is big enough, the facts do not count. The dream is your rocket fuel towards success. The dream is your WHY, your REASON or PURPOSE in life.

SHEILA'S SPARKS: When Your Dreams Are Bigger Than Your Fears, You've Earned Your Degree From The University of Dreamology. (Proverbs 29:18) says: Where there is no vision, the people will perish."

Your dreams or visions are the gifts that God gave specifically to you. There will always be other people who may not see your dreams or visions as viable or attainable. They are looking at how you are today, and they cannot gaze into the future and see how you can transform your life using the power of your dreams or visions.

These people are non-believers, haters, naysayers, or people who want you to succeed, as long as you don't pass them up or leave them behind. You cannot take everyone on your journey toward success. Some people will, some will not, some do, and some do not take action to achieve success. Other groups are the want to doers, the going to doers, and the never-doers. Do not let anyone slow you down or steal your dreams. Rest if you must, but do not you quit!!!

To achieve your dreams, you must identify your gifts. Your gift is something that you have been doing as a hobby for free. By identifying your gifts, you will be better suited to achieve your dream, and you can turn your passion into profit.

SHEILA'S SPARKS: Don't Retire Re-Fire Your Visions, Goals, And Dreams.

We have been playing in the game of life, trying to figure life out ourselves, even during retirement. How has that worked out so far? (James 4:2) says: "Ye have not because ye ask not." That is so profound. We can ask God for the desires of our hearts, dreams, or visions to manifest into our daily 'lives in just a few moments of prayer.

Do not quit on achieving your dream!!! Even if you do not have the money to fund your plan. If you do not have the ideal family to support your vision, do not stop believing or quit. You may not have the impressive, picture-perfect background that you see in soap operas. You may not have prestigious friends in your circle of influence. Do not give up on your dreams.

Prayer is a direct form of communication with God. Before, during, and after you pray, do you believe that your prayers will manifest? Do you have the unwavering faith that you will live your dreams and see your visions manifest into reality? Do not block your Blessings by not believing in the power of your dreams, ideas, and prayers.

SHEILA'S SPARKS: After Prayer, You Cannot Sit Back Down On The Couch And Lift The Heavy Remote Control, Watching

Television And Eating Potato Chips All Day Long And Expect A Miracle To Happen. (Proverbs 13:4) says: "Laziness wants it all and gets nothing, but the energic have something to show for their lives."

Achieving your dreams may be twice as hard and may take you twice as long. You may not read as fast as the next guy. You may not comprehend what you read without asking a question, after question, for clarity and understanding. You may go after your dreams over and over, and over again, having little to no success. Whatever you do, do not quit until achievement or death – whichever comes first.

Think back, regardless of your age, to some of the lowest points in your life. Did you say O' Lord and proceeded to explain your problems and ask for solutions? Did you pray about it while withholding your misery deep inside of your mouth, dare not telling another living soul?

During your prayers, did you share your vision with God about how you viewed the outcome of your prayer? Did you share your dream of changing things and living a better lifestyle? Did you indicate how you can help and serve others?

Even in your Re-fire, retirement years, you still have unfulfilled prayers that God can answer. You have dreams that you want to experience. You have visions to turn into reality. But, at any age when the goal is big enough, the facts do not count.

In this life here on earth, you must go through trials, tribulations, great suffering, but do not quit. It may be more challenging than you thought it would be, but do not quit. Instead, transform your mindset from despair and defeat and tell yourself, "I don't quit, I'm a winner, can't nobody, not even me, can't steal my dream." Every finisher/winner has felt the urge to quit somewhere along their journey in life, but they did not give up.

There may be close calls, but do not quit. Do the best you can with what you have. Learn to hang on in there. You were born to win. We need to confess what we want to possess. There is a unique positive mental attitude and thought process connected with winning. What you think about you bring about. When you start paying attention to your thoughts, you can cause a change in your behavior. When you change your behavior, you can change your life.

How are you responding to your thoughts? Do you self-evaluate how you think, feel, and act? Are you guiding your thoughts in the direction of achieving that special something that you desire? Or are you playing the woe is me blame game, victim card, about why you have not accomplished your dreams? Intentional thinking is where the power of self-actualization, the realization or fulfillment of your talents, along with your untapped potential, can become your driving force for achievement.

SHEILA'S SPARKS: What You Think About Is What You Bring About.

What you think about grows. God knows your good, bad, right, or wrong thoughts and issues. So why not be honest with yourself. When things are out in the open, you bring them out of the darkness and into the light. Do not get stuck in guilt, shame, and self-condemnation. You cannot afford to get mentally down.

Les Brown – "If you fall, you might as well land on your back. If you can look up, you can get up."

Technology has been a significant contributor to how society is becoming less and less physically connected. Instead, society is becoming more increasingly virtually connected with the help of technology. Using technology requires using our minds on a higher level instead of having face-to-face, in-person interactions. Especially since safeguards against the coronavirus pandemic are in place, technology helps connect ability from one to one, more attainable, just as if we were in person.

Research says it takes 21 days to shape or change a habit. However, according to Phillippa Lally; a health psychology researcher at the University of London, during my internet search for information, new habits usually take a little more than 66-days, or 2-months to develop, and as long as 254 days until it's fully formed, and ready for routine implementation.

Pour the right amount of presentence and positive energy into developing your habits, and your actions will dictate your achievements. It is challenging work; whether it be 21-days or 66-days, it is worth setting the correct habits needed for your success. Vladimir Horowitz said: "The difference between ordinary and extraordinary is practice."

<u>SHEILA'S SPARKS:</u> Your Habits Can Be Your Greatest Helper or Your Heaviest Burden. Your Habits Will Either Drag You Down To Failure or Lift You Toward Success.

The Law of Attraction states that positive or negative thoughts bring positive or negative experiences into those thoughts. Therefore, you must construct a positive message, telling yourself not to quit.

Life will keep going in an aimless direction until you decide to be the captain of your thoughts. Proceed as if the GPS guiding system now maps your mind. (Romans 12:2) says: "And be ye not conformed to the world but be ye transformed by the renewing of your mind." That focused attention on positive transformation can bring the desired energy and frequency level needed to make the difference and become a game-changer.

Do not be complacent or indecisive; stay strong, do not give up. Hard times do not last, but tough people do. If the plan did not work, revise it, and do not quit.

Think back before going on a road trip by car. You planned and mapped out your route before leaving. Along your journey, you run into detour signs. Now you must take a different, unplanned course to arrive at the same destination. This route takes you about an hour out of your way. However, you arrive at your destination. Why? Because you did not quit, turn around, and go back home because of the detour.

So it is in life, when you reach a detour on your road to achievement, change your plan, map out a new route, and keep going. Winners never quit, and quitters never win.

CHAPTER THREE

REDISCOVER YOURSELF

We live in a day when people try to discover who they are, what they like, and what they want to achieve. It is interesting because we come into life with an identity. We are all children of God whether we acknowledge it or not. God has given everyone unique gifts and talents that are unique to them.

It does not matter whether you were born in a hut, small village, or into a life of glamour and splendor. God knows every person from the womb to the tomb of His creation.

(Psalm 139:15) says: "My substance was not hid from Thee, when I was made in secret, and curiously wrought in the lowest parts of the earth. (Psalm 139:16) says: "Thine eyes did see my substance yet being imperfect and in thy book all my members were written, which in continuance, were fashioned, when as yet there was none of them."

Reconnecting to a relationship with God helps us to understand how formidable we are. In some cases, it is easy to blend in with the crowd rather than become vulnerable from judgment or acting differently by acknowledging God. Rediscovering yourself may cause you to examine your feelings and the direction your spiritual life is going.

Take a stroll through your mind, think back, and remember things you liked and enjoyed doing. Maybe you enjoyed going on a nature walk, watching your favorite television series, or taking a long bath, for example. Give yourself time to redefine what you like and what you do not like. Now consider making the change, then start moving forward again doing what you want to do.

Begin to journal and write down whatever comes to mind. Then, using the steam of consciousness mindset approach, journal your awareness, focusing on your rational thoughts as little as 5-minutes daily may be sufficient therapeutic actions. Free your mind and thought process from distractions because you must focus on who you are and what you want to achieve.

When going through the rediscover yourself process, you may become uncomfortable with some of the self-actualization realities that no longer serve you along your journey of refiring your life. In other words, take a stroll through your mind and see what you find. Write down the good, the bad, and the ugly things about yourself. Write down the things that you want to eliminate from your life.

Now, it is time for you to set new goals that will empower you to change how you look at things; like, eating healthier, exercising more, and socializing with positive friends. Maybe go on an adventure or vacation or do something that gives you a sense of direction and a purpose-driven life: Set long-term and short-term goals for yourself.

Give yourself a short-lived celebration as a reward when you accomplish a goal. Then move on to the next. Embrace good, wholesome relationships that add value to your life. More importantly, keep your distance and stay away from toxic, unhealthy relationships. Stay away from people who constantly complain and do not offer up solutions to help elevate the issue or problem.

<u>SHEILA'S SPARKS:</u> People Are Either Part Of The Problem, Or Part Of The Solution.

When you are on a journey of rediscovering yourself, it helps to have positive, supportive, loving people around you.

Sometimes you cannot distance yourself from someone physically. However, you can distance yourself mentally and emotionally by not engaging or giving energy to the negativity.

Other people's negativity does not have to be your burden to carry. Their negativity reflects their shortcomings, not yours. If you keep a positive mental attitude, you are well on your way to being part of the solution.

Keep what when on in the past, back in the past! When looking back in the review mirror of your past life, you will see things that are a remarkable memory or a terrible reminder. Use the terrible reminders from your past as examples of what not to repeat in the present. Use the good memories as examples of doing the right thing.

Value yourself and who you are becoming in the present moment. In rediscovering yourself, it is essential to understand what your values are.

If there is a conflict between your positive thoughts, feelings, and actions and the negative thoughts, feelings, and actions, this may be a roadblock standing in your way of rediscovering yourself.

(Jeremiah 29:1,3) says: "For I know the thoughts that I think towards you sayeth the Lord, thoughts of peace and not of evil to give you an expected end." Do not let the thoughts of rediscovering yourself after all these years paralyze what you can still offer the world. God had not given us the spirit of fear but of love, power, and a sound mind. You owe it to yourself to continue to discover things about yourself.

Use your imagination. It is an incredible force that can create new paths for you and turn the 'impossible' into 'possible.' When used with purpose and intention, you can help make this world a better place because you continue to give the world your best.

Here is a short story for you?

I took a painting class with a group of friends, and I did not realize that I would enjoy myself as much as I did. I also discovered a new passion for media. Socrates said that an unexamined life is not worth living. I always had a servant leadership, heartfelt mindset. After rediscovering myself, I realized what I wanted to do. I loved serving and tapping into other people's gifts and talents.

That is WHY I got into the television, film, media industry. I get the opportunity to support people who God has blessed with unique skills, gifts, and talents. I get to help, serve, direct, and empower people to get in front of the lights, camera, action so that they can touch and impact more lives. When I look back at that moment of clarity and rediscovery, I realize it put me on a track to fulfill my purpose-driven life's destiny in my retirement years—end of the story.

I do not know where you are in life today. But I do now know if, in some way, life has taken you off course. I do not know if you have reached a stopping point of not knowing what to do next. But I do want to encourage you never to give up.

SHEILA'S SPARKS: Rediscovering Means Identifying Your Hidden, Untapped Gifts And Talents.

George Elliot said: "It is never too late to be what you should have been." Or to be what you could have been. Or become the person that God created you to be. But, rediscovering also means setting the reset button and expanding your career to do the things you love and are enthusiastic about in life.

There may be more to you than you are giving yourself credit for, so keep going and keep growing. We are all humans trying to live this earthly life. Be tolerant with yourself and others in their discoveries. Aristotle said: "Knowing yourself is the beginning of all wisdom." To know yourself is an important skill. When you know who you are, you know what you need to do instead of looking for permission from others to do what you already know you ought to do.

It allows you to bypass frustration caused by wasting time doing the wrong things. Once you know who you are, you will become more confident and understand your purpose. You will realize that you can continue to make and leave a more significant impact in the world. Tre Chalmers Brothers said: "Observing yourself is the necessary starting point for any real change."

Sometimes, who we are is different than who we want to become. Knowing who you are is so important. Your gift fits in a bigger picture of your journey to help you rediscover yourself.

You might have trials and errors in your discovery process, but do not give up before you cross the finish line marked for achievement. Focus more on your passion. Your passion produces effort, and continuous effort produces results. Focusing on your strengths gives you needed traction to begin making a bigger and better impact and difference in the world.

Michelangelo said: "The greater danger for most of us lies not in setting our aim too high and falling short but setting our aim too low and achieving the mark."

Rediscovering yourself can take time and patience. Yet, we are on a lifelong journey towards achievement. We constantly learn increasingly more about ourselves as we age and deal with life's highs and lows. Since there is not a one shoe fits all approach to rediscovering yourself, it can be hard to identify. However, being aware of your thoughts, feelings, actions, goals, and dreams can undoubtedly help push you in the right direction.

Try not to respond with an automatic reaction to things that bother you. Some people close to you, like family members or hecklers, know how to push your tolerance button and get specific responses from you. Instead, keep your positive mental attitude and always stay focused.

What do you get fired up about in life? What tugs at your heart strings? That is where your focus and attention should go.

Rediscovering yourself may not always be easy. It can be helpful to talk to an outside professional to help steer you along the way. For example, a therapist often asks, how do you feel? Questioning by a qualified therapist can help you get in touch with your deep feelings from within your thoughts. Cognitive-behavioral therapy can teach you how to talk to yourself more effectively. Interpersonal therapy can help you learn how your family influenced you and how you can choose effective relational patterns as an adult.

Figuring out your mental, emotional, personal, and business needs while choosing the appropriate type of therapy based on your needs is critical for helping you to rediscover yourself. Rediscovering yourself is about being your authentic self, being happy and fulfilled.

SHEILA'S SPARKS: Do Not Give Up On Yourself Or Your Dreams.

Align yourself with principles that will help you to excel in rediscovering yourself. Whatever you do not know or understand like it says in (Romans 8:28). "And we know that all things work together for good to those who love God, and to those who are called according to His purpose."

Start right where you are today. Think about the things you are already doing that you are good at regardless of pay. Think about the unique qualities needed for you to be effective. Henry David Thoreau said: "What you get by achieving your goals is not as important as what you become by achieving your goals."

Rev Johnnie Coleman said: "If it is to be, it is up to me." And Ruth Casey said: "It only takes one person to change your life, <u>YOU!</u>

CHAPTER FOUR

IT'S NEVER TOO LATE

It's never too late means that it is not impossible to do something regardless of how old one is. The phrase, 'It's never too late' is used to encourage you not just to try but to do whatever it takes to accomplish that special something that your heart desires.

I want to share a quick story about how circus elephants get physically and psychologically trained to give up and comply. As you read the following short narrative, ask yourself this question. Do I have the give-up mindset forced upon me, like the circus elephant, even though I have complete control over my thoughts as an adult?

When baby circus elephants are small, mentally, and physically weak, the trainer ties one leg to a rope with a wooden stake spiked into the ground. From the beginning, the baby elephant tries, and tries, and tries to break away physically, but the rope is too strong. Her leg begins to hurt, and her efforts to escape become few over time.

After days, weeks, and months, sometimes up to a year of physically failing to break away, the baby elephant's mindset is conditioned with the 'I cannot imagine breaking away mindset' that there is no escape. So, it is now impossible and gives up (quits).

As the mentally broken baby elephant grows into a physically powerful, six or seven-ton adult, despite her enormous strength, she allows her thoughts from her childhood to convince her that she still cannot break away. She is physically strong enough to rip the wooden stake out of the ground with a slight tug from her powerful leg. However, her 'I cannot break away mindset' is dominant over her desire to break free.

So, for the remainder of the strong, empowering adult circus elephants' life, she never achieves her dream of breaking away because of her 'I can't do it' thoughts that were embedded in her mind when she was a baby—end of the story.

What is it that is holding you back from mentally breaking away and refiring your life? Be honest with yourself. What emotional baggage blockers are you carrying around from your childhood that contribute to your limiting beliefs? Many adults suffer from experiencing the baby circus elephant syndrome well into adulthood. They still have the 'I can't do it' emotional baggage within their thoughts, minds, body, and souls. But, as humans, unlike the circus elephant, we can Re-Fire our emotional baggage and decide that yes, 'I can do it,' despite anything. When you change the way you think about things, the things you think about change.

Now compare the attitude and mentality of the circus elephant to that of the Lion. The Lion is known as the King of the Jungle. Why? Unlike the circus elephant, the Lion is not afraid of doing her thing. The lion is not afraid of going in her own direction (even in captivity). The lion is bold, courageous, fearless, and outgoing. The question is: Are you going to live your life with the circus elephant mentally or develop the mentality of the Lion/The King of the jungle?

Whatever your dream is, you must have the mindset that it is never too late to Re-fire your life. Some people might think they are too old (like the adult circus elephant) to break away and achieve their dreams.

The truth is, rediscovering your life has no expiration date. If only the strong, empowering adult circus elephant knew the truth about what she could do instead of focusing on what she thought she was unable to do.

<u>SHEILA'S SPARKS:</u> Are Your Thoughts Holding You Back From Achieving Your Dreams (fixed mindset vs. growth mindset)?

Many successful people did not achieve or start working on their dreams until their late 50s, 60s, or later in life. The following examples are of people who Re-fired their goals later in life.

At age 52, Ray Kroc started his first McDonald's. At age 52, Morgan Freeman landed his first major movie roles when he acted in Lean on Me, Driving Miss Daisy, and Glory, all in the same year. At age 61, actress Judi Dench made her Hollywood breakthrough when she played the role of M (James Bond Boss) in the James Bond 007 film, GoldenEye. Finally, at age 65 (when most people are retiring), Colonel Sanders Re-fired his life and achieved success when he founded Kentucky Fried Chicken.

Many people go to their grave, never discovering their purpose-driven life or reason for living. Les Brown said: "The graveyard is the richest place on earth because it is here you will find all the hopes and dreams that were never fulfilled."

When you know your purpose, you will fuel your reason for being here in this world. Retirement is not about just existing from day today. Life has meaning and has always been explored by adventurous people, from the creation days of Adam and Eve.

Some notable examples of people who have explored life are not limited to the following. Marco Polo explored the silk road to China. Charles Darwin explored Brazil, Argentina, and Chile. Ferdinand Magellan became the first European explorer to cross the Pacific Ocean. And Jean Baptiste Point DuSable explored fur trade routes and founded the City of Chicago.

Matthew Henson explored and was the first person to reach the top of the North Pole. Bessie Coleman studied aviation and became the first African American woman to make a public flight. And Woni Spotts explored traveling and became the first African American woman to visit every country in the world by visiting 195 recognized nations, all seven continents, and twenty-two territories.

Two examples of modern-day explorers are: In 2021, Sir Richard Branson, 71-years old (Virgin Galactic), launched and successfully explored the edge of space onboard his Virgin Galactic rocket plane. In 2021, Elon Musk, 50-years old (SpaceX), launched the first privately owned capsule carrying NASA astronauts to the space station and back.

I went into detail about exploration because the many different creations within our universe have a purpose. I want you to realize that you can explore life on whatever level your interest is. You do not have to be like any of the people mentioned above. However, once again, "Life is meant to be explored."

You can explore tasting different foods while experiencing diverse cultures. In addition, you can explore museums, art galleries, your local state park, various genres of music, or learning a new language.

SHEILA'S SPARKS: Exploration And Discoveries Are The Keys To Advancing Our World And Humanity.

I want to share another quick story with you.

I will give you a glimpse of what motivates me. I never thought about authoring a book before, but it was a discovery that I explored about myself in my later years. It is exciting that I do not have to be a coach potato, using the remote control to exercise my fingers.

I now understand not to use my age as an excuse. It is never too late to Re-Fire your life after redefining your options. So, developing my, I can do it, positive mental attitude, I became a Film and Television Producer. I became a Vice President of an Animation Company, a Podcast Show Host. A Co-Owner of a Book Company, a Certified Life Coach-teaching Neuroscience Technology, the President of a Non-For-Profit Organization, and the author of two books.

All because it is never too late to Re-fire one's life. God wants us to use every gift available. Your gifts & talents are not just for you. They are given to you for others to benefit from your service. When you do not play full out, others will suffer in our universe because you did not give your all.

Some people have so much to give in their later or golden years. When you look in the mirror of your life, you cannot fool or trick the reflection looking back at you. Understand what options you have available and make the best of what you have.

Once your options are clear, your choices will become limitless during the evaluation stage of decision-making.

Remember, negative energy can be toxic. Activate your positive energy and your positive mental attitude. It is never too late to understand your next move. With a well-thought-out plan of action, the only thing remaining for you to do is take action ASAP.

Fortify and strengthen your mind and heart against malicious attacks against you and your abilities. When you do what others don't and experience the success that others won't, you become a target for the lazy, hatters, and naysayers. You know the type (gossipers).

There is spring, summer, fall, and winter seasons. But there is also your due season for greatness. Do not keep holding yourself back—no more holdups, delays, or excuses. Do not settle for less when you can achieve a better best. Do not tell yourself you have missed your chance, or you are on the clock. It is never too late to Re-Fire your life and live your dreams.

You are not a failure because you do not have a degree. You are not a failure if you have not married by age forty-five. You are not a failure if you do not own your own home by age fifty. You are not a failure if you have not figured out how you want to Re-fire your life at age sixty. Your chance of success has little to do with your age. Success in life is whatever you define it to be.

We all succeed at different timelines, and that is okay. It is never too late to learn something new. From life lessons (street-ology-never attending college) to high school graduation or getting your GED. It is never too late to get your college/university degree or take the entrepreneur route.

It is not too late for you to travel the world or become an accomplished cook/chef and get your culinary degree. It is not too late to pursue a passion project. You do not have to use age as an excuse.

Have you heard the word excusitis? It means anyone who is carrying emotional baggage filled with limiting beliefs that causes them to make excuses for not being, having, or doing the right thing to refine and Re-fire your life." Once again, age is not an excuse for not being, doing, and having achieved your heart's desire.

You are more than capable of learning and achieving something worthwhile. Even after physical growth stops, mental and emotional growth keeps happening. As we age, life gives us more time to explore the achievement of our dreams. Committing to personal development and growth as you age can help you age gracefully.

It is never too late to fall forward. One thing is for sure, we all will never stop making mistakes as long as we keep trying. Making mistakes is an unavoidable part of life. Making mistakes is how we learn. Making mistakes is how we grow. The only person who never makes a mistake is the person who never tries anything.

After making the mistake of touching a hot stove, you will never do that again. Mistake made; lesson learned. Falling forward means adapting to favorable change, building a healthy store of resistance, and learning to be resilient in the face of adversity. People who make mistakes know how to use those experiences to propel them towards success.

Here are a few more quick short stories!!!

Thomas Edison's teachers told him he was too stupid to learn (a form of the circus elephant syndrome). Edison got fired from his first two jobs for being nonproductive in the working world. That was not his desire or passion. As an inventor, Edison did not fail. He made 1,000 attempts (mistakes) before he successfully perfected the lightbulb.

George Washington Carver made many mistakes before he developed over three hundred product uses for the tiny peanut. Being successful to you may not be about personal fulfillment or about winning awards. However, as they get older, most people may obsess about not achieving success. Looking back on their life, they might feel disappointed.

There have never been more millionaires than there are today. Do not spend too much time on unimportant tasks. If you need to change anything, change your perspective about how you spend your time and with whom you spend your time.

Ask for wisdom, specialized knowledge, and understanding to help you along your way. These three words will function as your guideposts along your mental highway of thought, with your destination being to not give up on your goals. Decide that you will not give up because your age is just a number. What you are seeking is also seeking you—the law of attraction works. But to make it work, there are specific action steps on your part that you must take.

You can create the reality that you want or desire. Your thoughts can become things when followed by action. You can become the thinker who creates the ideas which make things happen. Practice being still while sitting in a quiet place. Clear the cobwebs from your mind while you begin to attract the Holy Spirit.

Channel your thoughts and energy in the form of prayer. Become tuned in, tapped in, and turned on to the power and presence of God.

SHEILA'S SPARKS: Your Spiritual Flow State Strengthens Your Belief And Faith That All Things Are Possible With God.

Look around the room that you are in while you are reading this book. Everything that you see, including the completion of this book, came from an idea or imagination from thought.

(Proverbs 3:5,6) says: "Trust in the Lord with all thine heart lean not unto thine own understanding, in all thy ways acknowledge Him and He shall direct thy path." (Proverbs 3:5,6) teaches us that we are not to depend on our understanding. Instead, we must trust God for guidance by acknowledging Him by keeping a moment-by-moment connection with Him through prayer.

God is not just concerned with our spiritual decisions; He also thinks about our choices that affect our everyday lives. The bible says faith comes by hearing. You must have a positive message to move forward and not give up. That is why the bible says: "To be ye transformed by the renewing of your mind." That focused attention can bring about the desired energy and frequency level needed to make the significant difference between the dash from birth and the dash until death, do us part this earth.

God is not finished with you because you are a senior-aged citizen. (Philippians 1:6) says: "Being confident of this very thing, that He which hath begun a good work in you will perform it until the day of Jesus Christ." Remember (Philippians 4:13) says: "You can do all things through Christ which strengthens you."

You are making the decision not to give up. It is not too late to strengthen your resolve. You are not defeated when you suffer temporary loss or setback. You are only defeated when you quit. A quitter never wins, and winners never quit! Do not get discouraged because of your age.

Many companies employed baby bloomers, who kept on swinging until they hit or produced the needed breakthroughs. Their companies and brands are still around today as proof positive that age is not a factor. Do not allow stereotypes, limiting beliefs, and false truths to hold you back from living your best life.

Thomas Edison – "Our greatest weakness lies in giving up." Do not allow someone else's failures to drag you down. You cannot control how others think, feel, and act, but you can control yourself. You are unique and one of a kind.

Put your trust in God. If He told you something, believe it is possible. (Proverbs 24:16) says: "The righteous may fall seven times but gets up, but the wicked will stumble into trouble. "Forget the past. Stop looking in the rearview mirror of your life. Think about why the front window of your future is larger than the rearview mirror of your past life. Is it because what happened in your past is not as important as what can happen in your future? It is not too late. You can still press onward towards the results that you seek.

CHAPTER FIVE

DEAL WITH THE ROOT NOT THE FRUIT

The bible says that the Lord God took (Adam) and put him in the garden of Eden to tend and keep it. That was Adam's job. Whatever God calls you to do, He will provide the gifts and talents. What God demands of you; He supplies in you.

Adam had it within him to do the work. God would not have told him to do something he was not capable of achieving. Whatever God expects of you, He injects in you. God is not dependent on us; we are dependent on God.

Dealing with the root means looking at the core beliefs, feelings, and thoughts that govern our behaviors. The root purpose is our thought process, mindset, emotions, attitude, and actions.

The fruit is the positive transformational results stemming from the root of your thought process. You can use your knowledge, wisdom, gifts, and talents to unpack and unlock the next phase of your life. You may be in a place or position in life where you thought, because of your age, your next dream was not possible because it was not deeply rooted and bared no fruit.

Let me share a short story with you.

On December 8th, 2020, Dr. James Dantley, the Host of the James Dentley show and the founder of JD3TV, and special guest co-host Michael Bart Mathews, Author and Founder of We Create Books, interviewed Brandon Steiner live on the James Dentley Show. During that interview, one of the questions to Steiner was: 'Will you describe how extraordinary achievement is similar to a tree?'

Steiner went on to say (I am paraphrasing), the trunk of the tree is commitment. The ROOTS are PURPOSE. The branches are passion, and the FRUIT & leaves are TRAITS that symbolize – Focus, Clarity, Creativity, Determination, Diligence, and Thoughtfulness. Understanding the power of the ROOT and the FRUIT is synonymous with having the same level of importance, enabling you to Retire and Re-fire your life.

Dealing with your ROOT (purpose) and your FRUIT (traits) for self-improvement are two empowering self-help and personal development tools that you can use not just to Retire but Re-fire your life.

There is a place in life where you are supposed to be, and it is not that same place when you were younger. It is a different destiny that calls you today. There are dreams that God has given you in your heart that you thought could not happen. The root purpose of your plan made you feel joyful. You saw new possibilities, and. The fruit is now plentiful. You are now full of life and hope.

As time passed on, the weeds of doubt began to grow and take root inside of your thought process. The weeds of doubt are now in competition with the seeds of belief within your mind. So now you have two types of roots growing in the same mental space within your thoughts—the weeds of doubts and the seeds of belief.

The weeds of doubt, if strong enough, can and will choke out the nourishment from your seed of belief or thoughts of 'I can do it.' Over time, because you did not wait to remove the negative roots, you allowed the weeds of doubt (thoughts) to choke out your good seeds of belief.

Those weeds of doubtful thought tell you that you are too old to begin again. The weeds of doubts will whisper in your ear, telling you that you cannot push the reset button.

SHEILA'S SPARKS: Will You Allow The Weeds Of Doubt (procrastination/failure) Or The Seeds Of Belief (action/achievement) To Be Your Dominant Thought Process? The choice is yours!!!

Here is another short story for you.

I have a friend named Rosie. We were having a conversation about her wanting to go back to school. She felt that in her forties, she was too old. She had several children, and she was a divorcee. She felt that her current position in life was her lot in life. However, she always wanted to be a teacher.

As she talked about her life-long dream, I asked her how old she was, and she said forty-four. I asked her again how long it would take her to reach her educational goals if she decided to go back to school, she said four years. Then, I asked her how old she would be if she did not go back to school in four years; she replied, forty-eight. Finally, I asked her if she went back to school, finished her education, and pursued her life-long dream job of becoming a teacher, how old would she be? She said the same age as before, forty-eight.

I looked her straight in the eyes and said, well, my friend, if you are going to be the same age with or without the degree, you might as well achieve it and be happy. She looked like she just experienced her aha moment, and she said, you are right. So, after finding her moment of clarity and discovering her power within, she went back to school, finished her education, and fulfilled a life-long dream—the end of the story.

The weeds of doubt within her mind were holding her back from becoming a teacher. However, she fulfilled her dream later in life. If your root thoughts are negative, your feelings can feel despair, lack faith and hope. You will not produce the juicy fruit of positive achievement.

Some weeds of doubtful thoughts (limiting beliefs) are: I'm all alone, I have no one to turn to for help. I am powerless, and I am not deserving, I am a failure, I do not belong, I am weak-minded. Having believed those kinds of weeds (limiting beliefs) from negative thought, how can transformation, change, and achievement be accomplished?

To clean out the seeds of doubt, we must deal with the root (thought process) because it relates to the obtainable juicy fruit of achievement. It is all about developing your positive mental attitude and mindset. Dealing with where your thoughts and beliefs came from is essential.

Many children received negative comments throughout childhood, like; you will never amount to anything because of their father, mother, education, color, or any other reason or excuse. If you believe that language, those negative comments can affect your positive mental attitude and personal growth.

I heard many people blame their failure on others because they believed the stories told to them in their youth. They listened to those sabotaging non-truths that affect many adults today. Reflect on the story about the baby circus elephant's belief. She did not have the mental capacity to free herself from the rope and wooden stake that held her captive throughout her adult life. Why? Because of how her mind was programed when she was a baby elephant.

The same philosophy exists in human behavior. There is a saying: If you hear a lie long enough, you eventually will begin to believe it. Therefore, positive affirmations are meaningful. We must counteract the negative messages spoken to us during our childhood, like the circus elephant's, I cannot break away syndrome of thought. The problem is that when we begin to believe things other people tell us, no matter who they are, we begin to form our own limiting beliefs.

People begin to struggle, feel ashamed, unworthy, rejected, and other self-defeating, limiting beliefs and behaviors. That mindset and thought process is a significant reason that holds them back from pursuing better options in life. The root of your positive thoughts and beliefs will determine the juicy taste of achievement from the fruits of your labor.

SHEILA'S SPARKS: People Will Blame Others For Their Inability To Achieve Their Goals And Dreams Rather Than Take Responsibility For Achievement Themselves.

I have heard young men blame not having a father in their life for their bad behavior. Sin and negative behavior were in the garden of Eden, in the bible. There is a common theme between the root and the fruit.

Let me share negative thinking in the garden of Eden (Genesis 3:1,7). Also, Jesus talked about the root of sin (John 8:44) and (Matthew 12:33-35, 15:18-19). The Apostle Paul spoke about the origins of evil in (Romans 1:25). There is a sinful behavior behind brokenness. Every negative thought or lie comes from Satan, the father of lies, and the lies become your negative root-based thinking system that produces a negative, deceitful identity and lifestyle.

So, we guard against being hurt again, rejected again, and betrayed again. We must search our identity for the righteous thoughts of our minds and feelings in our hearts, like root thoughts that tempted Christ to think negative. God can reveal your lies. God can also release you from your lies and replace your lies with His peace, His truth, His victory, His purity, and His righteousness. God can give us a new, reborn again identity.

It does not matter who you answered to over the years. God gave Abraham, Sarah, Jacob, and Paul name changes, which came with new identities.

God can give you a brand-new identity. Every mental attack is an attack against our most faithful, deepest identity as God's sons and daughters. Jesus experienced many suffering that humanity experiences today. Nevertheless, Jesus was victorious, and the feeling of our infirmities touched him. Jesus experienced struggle. He asked God to help him when he was in the garden of Gethsemane praying.

He experienced abandonment by close friends. He experienced betrayal by a kiss from Judas. Jesus experienced verbal and physical abuse when they beat him before going to the cross. He experienced temptation by people who wanted him to drink, to numb his pain, yet he refused it. Jesus experienced rejection by His Father when he cried out; why have you forsaken me on the cross. Finally, Jesus experienced unfair treatment when he was falsely accused, tried, convicted, and crucified.

Jesus held every thought captive in his mind. He did not allow the root of belief to cause bad fruit of thoughts and behaviors. Jesus can relate to our seeds and roots of thought. As I said earlier, he was a suffering Christ.

Jesus can identify with people whose parents were unwed because his mother was unwed at the time of his birth. He was a refugee for a while, and he felt alone and abandoned by close friends. Jesus knew what it was like to be betrayed by others. He knows what it was like to be stripped naked, physically, verbally, and mentally violated by religious leaders.

He knows what shame, humiliation, and embarrassment are. He knows what it is like to feel suffering and pain. He knows what it is like to be arrested, convicted, and sentenced to death row. He knows what guilt and regret feel like. Jesus can identify with us human beings in many areas. Remember, negative thoughts and feeling produces negative experiences.

God can guide us by helping us focus on Christ-centered, cross-centered, word-centered, and God-centered behaviors. (Jeremiah 33:3) says: "Call to me, and I will answer you, and show you great and mighty things, which you do not know."

There is a cycle from Root to Fruit. First, it is like sin and forgiveness. In other words, it is like the thought, I am alone (negative belief/root thought), which could produce fearful emotions, feelings, and negative behaviors, which may make you feel less joyful or peaceful. Next, you begin to trust in your efforts to find comfort.

Meaning you are trying to find a quick antidote. For instance, a person feels lonely or sad (a root thought) that produces negative feelings and begins binging while eating ice cream or other food that you may not need. So, your negative actions create the food eating disorder behavior. This behavior makes you feel temporary instant gratification because you trusted your efforts to find comfort.

But avoiding God and His grace at that moment reinforced a negative pattern of thoughts, feelings, emotions, and behaviors. We can talk to God about our negative thoughts, feelings, behaviors, addictions, and compulsions open and honestly. We can immediately and continually ask God to release and replace the lies from Satan, the father of lies. We can also ask Him to reveal when Christ faced the same kind of negative thoughts that we may have.

SHEILA'S SPARKS: We Can Do Nothing Using Our Strength, Apart From Christ.

We can focus on our performance and receive His glory. (Matthew 7:17-18) says: "A good tree cannot bring forth evil fruit, neither can a corrupt tree brings forth good fruit." Our developmental assignment is to figure out our good tree-rooted positive thoughts and feelings and separate them from the evil tree-rooted negative thoughts and feelings that we might have experienced when we were younger.

I am sure you heard random conversations about how people slow down because they are getting older. They kick back, relax, take it easy, live a rocking chair lifestyle because they lived your life. So, they think there is no need to reach out or keep dreaming big and believing in yourself and what new goals you can accomplish.

You might have heard things about retirement and how life is almost up. Whatever your self-sabotaging root thoughts and feelings were throughout your life, you can control your life by controlling your mind in your retirement years. Now, your assignment is for you to seek out where Jesus can identify with you and your story.

Jesus had stepbrothers and sisters that had feelings about him that were not always positive. So whatever deep-rooted, negative thoughts or beliefs you have about getting older, replace your thoughts with positive thoughts and affirmations. We do not have to feel stuck at retirement. Refiring (changing our thoughts) also means Christ walking in and through us while He grows us in His grace. Maybe your dreams have been put on hold for years because you were busy building your boss's dreams by working a job for years and years.

Your fellow man may have forgotten you, but God has never forsaken you. God leaving a gift in you is the fact that He has not forgotten you. It is a reminder that what He has purposed for your life is going to happen. Age is nothing but a number, as my mother used to say. Even if you did not get paid what your gift was worth, do not be deceived by the surface because God can still bless you.

Do not let your net-worth determine your self-worth. Your blessing can come in many different forms, just as the greatest treasures on earth are in many various forms. People might look over you because of your age, but that is all right. Your greatest treasures and value are called your experience, knowledge, and wisdom. And that, my friends, comes with age.

Older generations (our senior citizens) have experienced many trials, tribulations, losses, roadblocks, and setbacks. Yet, capitalization from their life experiences, they gained wisdom-related knowledge about handling challenges and problems versus their much younger, inexperienced generations that have yet to endure those same experiences.

Continue to nurture and share your gifts are in full force. The world needs your skill sets. God never creates a gift inside of you that lacks service to others. The fact that you have a skill God put inside of you means that an audience is waiting to receive it.

Do not become discouraged because of your age!!! Please do not give up on your special gift regardless of your many years of serving people who were not ready to receive it. They were not the people that God called you to help and serve. Stay the course until you find the people who need the type of gift or service God has placed inside you.

Remember, all fish do not eat all bait. I remember going fishing with my brother (who loves to fish); I saw he had various bait for catching fish. He said: "You can fish in the wrong waters with the wrong type of bait, assuming that your bait is no good, but when you cast your line in waters with fish that does not eat your bait, you must move to another watering hole.

Man's rejection of thinking 'you are not good enough' is God's direction to keep you moving towards better opportunities. God is not moving you backward in life as you grow older. Instead, he is moving you forward towards more.

Greater is the accomplishment of your season of dreams that you have put on the back burner for years. Do not let your senior years in life allow you to think that you cannot or will not discover your dreams, and there is no harvest coming. The length of wait for your blessing from your harvest determines the magnitude of how you plant, water, nurture, and till the rich mental soil (thought process) around your seed (mindset) of growth.

God has you, He is not panicked, and neither should you. He said He would not leave you or forsake you. Do not count God's silence as absence. God is the one that makes all dreams come true. God will give you a need for your special gift that He has for you to share with others. You have not reached the age you are by accident, coincidence, or by chance. God has brought you to this season in your life for a reason.

He has brought you to this season in your life with purpose, for a purpose, and on purpose. So be able to confirm things that He has spoken in your heart. Every dream that God has spoken to you. You can achieve every goal in your heart.

Napoleon Hill – "Whatever the mind of man can conceive and believe it can achieve." Hill never mentioned you must be a certain age to experience achievement. Instead, he said you must conceive and believe before you can achieve.

God can send the rain to water the root and bring up good fruit in your season. However, sometimes people must transform their mindset to maintain the 'I can do it' positive mental attitude in their older season of life.

There is a term called 'backsliding' in the church. That is when you let go of God's principles and live a life of a worldly person that does not follow God's teaching or instruction according to the bible. Well, 'front sliding' is when the devil promotes you before your character develops and is strong enough to share your positive mental attitude and gift with others. So, let us be patient and allow your age, knowledge, wisdom, and experience to work for you. Then, allow God to enable you to live your dreams in your senior years.

God specializes in taking older people and making young dreams come alive. So, think back and reclaim your dreams. Is there anything too hard for God? It would help if you accelerated your effort toward achieving your goals. Fortunately, God has a more significant schedule for your life. Just like the farmer plants seeds in the ground to grow the mighty Oak Tree, God can increase your harvest using the seeds from your positive mental attitude.

<u>SHEILA'S SPARKS:</u> It Is All About Mindset, Developing Your Positive Mental Attitude, And Believing You Can Achieve Your Heart's Dreams And Desires.

Do not sit on the tarmac before takeoff doing nothing. Self-help and personal development tools are available to assist you in developing the right mindset.

Og Mandino – "I will persist until I succeed. I was not delivered unto this world into defeat, nor does failure course my veins."

Zig Ziglar – "You can have everything in life that you want if you just help other people get what they want."

Use your gifts in this stage of your life to help and serve other people. Your wisdom, knowledge, experience, and understanding in life are an asset. You have learned from life's lessons, disappointments, bumps in the road, setbacks, and failures that you have encountered. You have skills and abilities. Reconstruct your mindset to look and explore the right fruit to change your life.

CHAPTER SIX

WHAT DO YOU MAKE OF YOUR SAGE?

A sage in classical philosophy is someone who has attained wisdom. The biblical term 'sage' is often translated as the wise. The sages were the actual leaders and teachers of the Jewish religion from the beginning of the second temple penned until the Arabian conquest of the east. When someone gives you sage advice, it usually means sounds, intelligent advice, coming from a wise or experienced person. Sage can be used to connect to the spiritual realm or enhance intuition.

Healers and laypeople in traditional cultures burn sage to achieve a healing state or to solve or reflect upon spiritual dilemmas. The Chinese refer to sage as someone above the common herd, of surpassing wisdom, and possessed of inability to act in an unimpeded, far-reaching manner. Webster's definition of sage: "One distinguished for wisdom, a mature or vulnerable person of sound judgment."

In the Grimm's fairytales, the brothers Grimm published classic stories in literature like; Hansel and Gretel, Cinderella, Rumpelstiltskin, Snow White, and the Seven Dwarfs, etc.

In their fourth edition of the Brothers Grimm, they have a thing called the duration. The story's synopsis is that God initially determined thirty years as the ideal life span for all animals, including humanity and the monkey. The dogs and the monkeys considered it much too long and begged God to reduce their years to eighteen, twelve, and ten being healthy, vicious, and greedy – man asked to be given those extra years, God agreed.

So, a man's life span totaled forty years. The first thirty years were his own, and they went extremely fast. The following 18 are the donkey years, during which he must carry countless burdens on his back, then come the dog years, twelve years when he can do little but growl and drag himself along—followed by the monkey years, which are his closing ten years. After that, he grows strange and does things that make children laugh at him.

People fear growing old. Never fear growing old, fear growing stale, as you grow old. Be afraid of losing a child-like active faith in God. Instead of praying if I should die before I wake, we should pray – wake me up before I die. A simple survey involved participants who were ninety-five years old. They volunteered to answer the following question. If you could live their life all over again, what would you do differently?

The top three answers. #1. I would reflect more, #2. I would risk more, and #3. I would do more things. These answers mean they would live a more purpose-driven, intentional life. They would have stepped out on faith much more and lived a life without regret.

What do you make out of the time you have been on this earth? There are many things to be discovered in life. Just think about the sky for a moment. If you were to go outside on a clear night with no pollution obstructing your view, what do you see when you look up in the sky? The bible says God has marked out the heavens with His span, meaning, as far as the eye can see, to infinity and beyond.

As we look up at the sky-blue canopy in search of the Heavens, we can trust God in the midst of whatever we are going through because He is in charge of it all. He created bigger things than your problems. God has it all under control. The sun, moon, stars, planets, and galaxies within the universe are all God's creations.

God promised Abraham children. He was one-hundred, and Sarah was in her nineties before they had a child. What do you think her Gynecologist would have said today to Sarah and Abraham?

Physically, it was impossible because she had always been barren. Natural impotence is nothing when put next to divine competence. We have a God that turns the impossible into possible. The word impossible means 'I'm possible.' The older you get, the wiser you should get because of your past lessons and many years of experience. Ridding ourselves of the bigotry of age discrimination helps our view of moving forward.

Personal development should continue throughout our lifetime. Do not be like the typical retiree that follows along like a line like sheep. Sheep are always following the leader, even to the slaughterhouse of death. They do not show any resistance; they fall in line and follow each other.

Be like the lion, who is a different breed. The lion earned the title King of the Jungle. Why? Because lions are fearless throughout their journey. They are not the largest animal, nor are they the smartest. However, they are feared the most and are the most daring of all the animals in the jungle.

The retirees that follow along in life like sheep are those people that have little to no goals and dreams after they retire. They did not Re-Fire their life!!! Those people that re-fire after retirement is like the lion, fearlessly going for their goals and objectives every day of their journey. Lions play full-out once they are in the hunt, letting nothing stop them.

Do not sleep with the sheep, be a lion. Shed the sheepskin wool off your back and replace it with the lion's distinctive mane. Think about your time here on earth and realize plenty of experiences and things yet to explore. Do not allow thoughts of your age or insecurities to hold you back from your journey. Remember, be like the lion, fearless and limitless!

A limited belief in yourself can hold you back from refiring your life. Do not allow others to make you feel unworthy or that you cannot make any more meaningful contributions. When you find your moment of clarity, you can use your God-given talent, knowledge, and wisdom to empower and serve others, regardless of your age.

You can strive to achieve excellence throughout your life when you harness the power of purpose. God gave man a vast amount of intellectual thought power for the sole purpose of decision-making. With the new never-ending improvement of human intelligence, great inventions come with new knowledge and experiments.

Refine your gifts and continue to use them. You can still be valuable to our global society. Dr. Martin Luther King: "You want to do your job so well that the angels lean over and say that you are the best at what you do." You are a masterpiece even at your current age because you are a piece of the master. You were born to think, create, invent, and serve people's needs. You are here for a reason.

<u>SHEILA'S SPARKS:</u> You Are Not A Mistake; You Were Born To Achieve Greatness.

God has that special something that he chose you to do. That is why you were born. God does not make junk.

When you understand who you are, where you come from, and why you are here on earth, you can transform your life. Every morning, people get up and go to a job they hate. Many of those same people stay on that job until they retire even though they hate it. The majority stayed on a job they did not like, working with people they did not like, and making less money than their worth, never knowing who, what, where, when, and why they existed.

Many employees did not know what they were supposed to do in life except go to work. So, they drifted along, becoming a wandering generality, taking on assignment after assignment, and never utilization their unique gifts and talents. As a result, they lived an unfulfilled life.

They did not know their mission or purpose. Employees worked the 40-40-40 plan. They were working 40-hours a week, for 40-years of their life, to retire on less than 40 percent of their income. On the other hand, many people re-fire their lives before they retire.

Most people never achieve their full potential in life. Imagine living 95 years and never understanding your potential or greatness.

The greatest tragedy in life is not death; it is living and not knowing your purpose. Without purpose, life does not have meaning.

Everybody wants to be successful. But God designed success to be predictable and achievable using your five senses. So, you do nothing, and nothing happens.

A seed planted from an Oak Tree will produce the mighty Oak Tree. The seed planted from a weed will grow weeds.

The mind of man will produce the mighty Oak Tree or weeds. It will grow whatever type of negative (weeds) or mighty (Oak Tree) seeds that you plant in your thoughts and allow those roots to grow within your mind. You are the caretaker of your thoughts. So be careful about what you plant in your mind. Because good, bad, right, or wrong, your thoughts will manifest into seeds of positivity or weeds of negativity.

The mighty Eagle symbolizes inspiration, the free spirit of the mind, victory/success, grace, speed, pride, longevity, and royalty. (Isaiah 40:31) says: "But they that wait upon the Lord shall renew their strength, they shall mount up wings of Eagles."

Having a positive mental attitude, like the characteristics of the mighty Eagle, success is sure to happen. Like the Eagle, we can leverage our like-minded positive thoughts, feelings, and actions. We are products of God, and He is our manufacturer. The manufacturer wants his creation (humanity) to be successful, just like the mighty Eagle.

SHEILA'S SPARKS: Re-Fire Don't Retire!!! Spread Your Wings Like The Mighty Eagle, Take Flight, Go After Your Dreams, Be A Symbol Of Inspiration To Others.

When you buy a television, you expect it to work correctly. When you get a new cell phone, you expect it to work according to the manufacturer's specifications. Products are created, designed, and comes with a manual. Our manual of instructions comes within the bible. We operate our product (thoughts) without consulting the manual (bible). When something goes wrong with a product, you are supposed to take it to an authorized dealer. In our case, "The authorized dealer is God" – Myles Monroe.

We often try to fix the product (ourselves) from unauthorized dealers (no spiritual guidance). Jesus Christ is an authorized dealer; you (humanity) are a product of God. The first thing He placed on you is His image. (Genesis 1:27) says: "In the beginning, God created in man His image, male and female created He them."

You are just like the manufacturer (God); that is why your failure is unpleasant for God. However, God does not hold a grudge against us for not following His principles. He still loves us.

SHEILA'S SPARKS: Stop Being Afraid To Dream. Reach Out, Dream Big – Believe In Yourself! Your success is good for God.

If we submit to the laws of God, then we will have success. God told Joshua the following in the bible.

Fish were created to swim in the water; birds were created to fly in the air. That is the law of nature. Birds will not try to live underwater, and fish will not attempt to live on solid ground. Those are the laws of nature.

Why did God create man? (Genesis 1:27) says: "So God created man in His own image, in the image of God created He Him; male and female created he them." (Genesis 1:28) says: "And God blessed them, and said unto them, Be fruitful and multiply, replenish the earth, and subdue it: and have dominion over the fish of the sea, and over the fowl of the air, and over everything living that moveth upon the earth."

According to Dr. Miles Monroe – "When we operate under the laws of God, we can have good success." Remember the scripture: "We were created by God, then blessed by God, and given dominion over every living creature on earth." Success is the result of having positive dominion over our decisions from thought.

Today, wherever you are in life stems from the negative or positive dominion over your thoughts, feelings, and actions. Failure in life is the result of decisions. Whatever you decide determines your destiny.

You become what you think about, and what you think about, you bring about.

George Elliot said: "It is never too late to become what you should have been, or what you could have been." Those are encouraging words! Your age is just a number. It does not have to be an obstacle preventing you from achieving your subsequent victory. Find another way to make it happen, be courageous, be resourceful, do not give up.

Robert Schuller said: "Tough times do not last, but tough people do." Wayne Gretzky said: "You miss 100 percent of the shots you never take." Do not lose sight of your dreams. Aim high, keep shooting toward your goals.

Awaken that burning desire that is deep, down inside of your mind, body, spirit, and soul. Connect with your positive mental attitude for achievement. Seek to understand your internal guidance system for success. Develop a profound, positive mental attitude and your core values. Finally, create the discipline that it takes to re-fire yourself at the age that you are today.

Do what you need to do. Get connections, resources, role models, or coaches to stay fired up towards achieving your goals. Get out of the life-altering situation of thinking it is all over. Stop thinking you are too old to use your gifts or dreams to contribute to the world.

Do not become paralyzed by self-sabotaging thoughts of being too old to help or serve society. Instead, tap into your inner self that says I can, and I will. Remember the bible says: "I can do all things through Christ which strengthens me." So here is one question for you to ponder: How old do you feel?

There is a Marist Poll that asked American adults if they thought age sixty-five qualified as old? Overall, two-thirds of the Marist Poll respondents considered sixty-five to be "middle-aged." My second question for you to ponder. If sixty-five years old is considered "middle-aged," would you agree that people aged sixty-five and older have time to Re-fire their life before Retirement?

SHEILA'S SPARKS: As You Grow Older; Don't Retire, Re-Refire.

CHAPTER SEVEN

OPPORTUNITY OR CRISIS

A crisis can become a time of intense difficulty, trouble, or danger. A crisis can be a dangerous situation affecting a group, individual, or all of society. A crisis can occur with little or no warning.

Most people's reactions to the word crisis are adverse. The COVID-19 global pandemic is or was a crisis, depending on when you are reading this book. The turmoil from the pandemic fallout is responsible for millions of deaths worldwide, millions of job losses, and millions of businesses going out of business. The breakdown of relationships, and in other cases, the lack of using common sense to stay safe are also contributing factors.

Several people view a middle-aged person behaving a certain way as experiencing a midlife crisis. Noticeable, out-of-the-ordinary changes in one's life can display signs of someone experiencing a problem. An emergency can become a radical change or status in a person's life.

Examples of a midlife crisis: Family disruptions or disturbances. Natural disasters, like weather-related incidents. Economic changes due to loss of a job. Not being able to pay the mortgage, rent, utility, and medical bills. Lack of adequate community resources like housing, food, crime protection, and even loss of a loved one.

We all know that a crisis can occur to anyone and does not matter what age you are. Unfortunately, a lot of people view getting older as a crisis. During these trying times, is when people feel helpless about the natural evolution of maturing.

Many seniors feel that their only alternative is to live on a fixed income. They can't see their way out of their economic situation, health, or physical situation. Having the limited income mentality may be true for some, but not for all.

People think when they are young that one day I am going to retire and travel. I will do what I want when I want and with whom I want to do it. But the reality is, there is no day on the calendar that is called one day. The decisions you make today determine your future outcomes. And those decision counts. Tomorrow never comes because we always wake up in the present (today). Abraham Lincoln said: "The best thing about the future is that it only comes one day at a time." One day your life will flash before your eyes; make sure it is worth watching. There are ways to deal with a crisis, and one of the best ways is to alleviate the cause as fast as possible. Do not sulk or stay in a rut or lash out at others. Instead, take stock of your life, and deal with your crisis. During an emergency, you must reprogram your mind, find your moment of clarity, and begin to think clearly. Remove distractions and obstacles that clutter your thoughts. Pray and ask for help from God and others. Look for manageable solutions. Work on positive crisis responses and focus on your priorities.

Utilize the resources that are available to you. Manage and take control of your thoughts. Lead by example. There is a saying between a manager and a leader. Managers do things right; leaders do the right thing. Think of people who lead by example, like Mahatma Gandhi, who spent his life living what he preached.

He was committed to nonviolent resistance to protest and injustice. Gandhi had millions of people who followed him. He created a picture of what was possible. Jack Welch of General Electric turned G.E. around by having everyone brainstorm and think of ideas for improvement instead of waiting for higher-ups. As a result, G.E. became an incredibly successful company under his management style.

Imagine, what if Martin Luther King had demonstrated violence in his marches but talked non-violence? His followers would have looked at him with suspicion and distrust because he spoke about non-violence yet practice something else.

Even Jesus did not ask us to do anything that he would not do. Instead, Jesus told us to take up our cross and follow him; he led by example. Facing a crisis cannot be unavoidable. When a problem does hit, it is easy to panic. However, it is crucial to remain calm and remember your plan for managing and managing the situation.

Life consists of moments of opportunities and crisis. A baby crying because of hunger, needing a diaper change, or a toddler crying in a store because they lost their parent, a student failing a course, a divorce, a death, or loss of a job are all crises.

But life also has moments of opportunity, and what we do with those opportunities matters. Today is your day of opportunity. Today is God's gift to you. How are you going to spend your time making an impact on Him? Your life was paid for with an unmatchable price when Jesus died for your sins. We must take advantage of the opportunities to do good and play full out. The bible says: "Let our lights so shine that others may see our good works."

We have moments of opportunities that come to us throughout our lifetime. When preparedness and opportunity meet, the by-product is a success. Sometimes, opportunity comes dressed up in work clothes. Have you heard people say: I am not going to work this or that job because it is not what I want? What we do with the opportunities God brings into our lives matters.

Sometimes we meet people, and they have a profound impact on our life. There are opportunities to achieve a higher level of success, improve our lives, and serve God in a greater capacity. Take advantage of opportunities even when you are older. Do not be afraid to seize the moment. Opportunities come and go.

<u>SHEILA'S SPARKS:</u> Opportunities Do Not Wait Around For The Fainthearted or The Doubting Thomas's.

Opportunities are all around us every day. You have an opportunity to get out of bed or stay in bed. Now whether you take advantage of the opportunity is your choice. For example, people like to eat and live well. So, they get out of bed, take advantage of their work or career, and get paid.

Sometimes people recognize an opportunity after someone else does it first. Then they think I wish I would have thought of that. Be sensitive to the open doors around you that God opens in the form of opportunities. (1 Corinthians 16:9) says: "For a great door and effective door has open unto me, and there are many adversaries."

Paul was speaking about a wide door of opportunities before him, but with adversaries. Your attitude and perspective about a situation have a lot to do with your outcome. When the Israelite children saw Goliath, they thought he was too big to kill. David saw Goliath, and he felt he was too big to miss! Same problem, unique perspective. What, is Goliath in your way? What is your view? Opportunities become realities to people who refine their lives with purpose and perspective. First, you must believe in yourself.

People believe a lie before they will believe the truth. The word 'believe' has the word (lie) in the middle of it. Fear will keep you from taking advantage of opportunities. Do not allow yourself to become stagnated by non-action because of fear. Someone once said, feel the fear, do it anyway.

Here is a short biblical story that I want to share with you about an opportunity to serve. It is a parable telling us how to treat people in three different ways. The first instance talks about a person 'getting robbed.' The robbers saw the man as prey. They are out to gain something. The second man, who was a priest, saw the man as trouble to avoid. So, he walked on past him. The third man, a Samaritan, saw the opportunity to minister to the man's needs. End of story.

Serving others is a spiritual discipline. There is such a thing as divine order and opportunity to those who believe. It may be a challenging reminder to follow the direction and guidance from God to serve others or be used by Him in some form. Are you taking advantage of the opportunities God sends you?

Re-firing your goals and dream is an opportunity to hit the reset button. Retirement is a time when you can still look towards achieving more goals and dreams in your life. Maximize the seconds, minutes, hours, days, months, and years of your life to the fullest—live life in your retirement years on purpose. Definite purpose is not what you do for a living. Definite purpose is what you live to achieve. Knowing your WHY is the key.

<u>SHEILA'S SPARKS:</u> Prepare, Prioritize And Be Prudent With Your Time.

Jesus spent years preparing and prioritizing His life. Yet, Jesus did not procrastinate or waste His time. So likewise, you were born for a purpose. You are here to discover, make use of, and share your multiple talents with others.

You cannot do, be, or have your heart's desires by remaining the same person you are today. You must first change the way you think, feel, and act. In other words, when you change the way you think about things, the things you think about change.

Understand that God does not subscribe to laziness or excuses. (Matthew 7:7) says: "Ask, and it shall be given you; seek, and you will find; knock, and it shall be opened to you." The words ask, seek, and knock are all action words. What does this mean? Those who subscribe to laziness by not asking, seeking, or knocking on the door of opportunity are blocking their blessings.

Let go of what is holding you back. God does not mention your negative past; the enemy within your mind does. That is why you must forget the negative past and move forward with your positive future. It is time to make the most of every opportunity God gives you.

Your positive mental attitude must be tuned in, tapped in, and turned on a higher frequency of thinking. Remember, laziness and excuses will always be opportunity stealers. Death does not issue refunds for unused time and talent not used. If you do not discover your unique gifts during your lifetime, your skillset will die with you.

If an opportunity presents itself to you as an open door, do not shut the door. Instead, pray for the courage to walk through it. In the middle of a tricky situation is an opportunity for you to decide the best course of action that can change your life. Through every adversity, there is a seed of possibility, depending on how you view the situation.

Some people think only lucky people have the best opportunities. However, anyone can have numerous options when your thoughts are tuned in, tapped in, and turn to the higher source. Also, by putting in the framework and preparing yourself for the opportunity, you will know when the time comes.

For you old-schoolers, Ann Landers said: "Opportunities are usually disguised as hard work, so most people don't recognize them." Decide what you want out of life and go after it with passion, feeling, and conviction. Excuses will always be there for you; the opportunity will not. Do not wait for what you feel is the right time. Instead, open your eyes, expect change, analyze the landscape, and take action.

Find ways to attract opportunities into your life. The more places you go, the more your name comes up, the more publicity you receive. The more people know you, your company, your product, and your service, the more opportunities will develop.

Suppose you do not understand how to get engaged with social media. Due to the coronavirus pandemic, a necessary shift in communication on a global scale has developed. Social media sites like Facebook, Twitter, Instagram, and blogging sites serve as opportunity door openers. Opportunities are everywhere for everyone prepared to receive it. You never know what might be awaiting you. Opportunities can increase exponentially, or opportunities can grow wings, take flight, and fly away forever.

Do not slow down your personal development transformational journey. Untapped opportunities are waiting for you. Look for trends, fill a need, and solve a problem. Be consistent with your core values. It will keep your drive going and carry your momentum toward achieving your goals. Make sure what you do adds value to others.

Retirement presents new opportunities to those who seek them. Of course, life is not perfect, but we can embrace each new day and decide to make it great.

SHEILA'S SPARKS: Don't Retire Re-Fire Your Opportunities!!!

Are you going to sit back in your lazy boy chair and let opportunities keep flying away? Are you going to keep doing the same thing while wanting, wishing, and praying for the desires of your heart to manifest within your life?

Success is the progressive realization of a worthwhile dream. HOW BIG IS YOUR DREAM? Along your Road 2 Eternity, the key is taking action. Remember ASK, SEEK, and KNOCK are all action words. This is a Skyward Books Presentation!!!

EPILOGUE

Now that you have read this book, you have more than enough spiritual examples and real-life antidotes to guide you along your journey of refiring your life through your retirement years. Each story in this book speaks to your thoughts, feelings, and emotional intelligence. The journey you are on begins with a positive mindset about your future.

My call to action for you is this: Please realize that you are still developing and growing every day when you look at life. Paying close attention to your personal development and self-help journey will keep you sharp. Use all your years of experience, knowledge, wisdom, and understanding to help you continue to accelerate your goals and dreams in the present and future.

Do not continue to do the same things in the same way and expect a different outcome. Instead, seek the help you need in the form of a coach, mentor, or a like-minded accountability partner who can help you blaze a new trail.

If you do not know something, begin asking questions. What will your legacy be? What will you be remembered for between the dash of life and your departure from death? Your memory or legacy depends on what you achieve based on the decisions you made or make to refire your vision, mission, goals, and dreams of achievement and service to others.

ABOUT THE AUTHOR

Sheila White is an award-winning film and television producer, writer, and author of her new book, "Discovering Your Uniqueness: A Young Person's Guide To Discovering Who You Were Created To Be."

She takes you on a journey of expanding your wisdom, knowledge, and understanding of how discovering your uniqueness is vital and the key to unleashing the seeds of greatness planted inside you at birth. Her latest work is the sequel of her debut book, "Don't Retire-Re-fire: Rediscovering Yourself in Your Later Years."

This book is full of inspiration designed to encourage you to find your moment of clarity as you harness the power of purpose. Sheila White is a recipient of the State of Illinois, Governor's Award for her drive and initiative for collaborating with breastfeeding moms and babies.

She has also received seven awards in film and television and has been featured in several magazines and newspaper articles, including Christian News Journal and the Joliet Business Magazine. In addition, Sheila has been a guest on different radio networks such as WJOL, WBGX, WHHN, and WLMN.

Sheila is also a segment Producer for a Chicago radio program The Lightning Strike and a Gospel Radio Host for Gospel On The Road produced by Road 2 Eternity Media.

She is the podcast host of her show: Gifted with Sheila White, and she is a self-discovery life coach who has received her training in neuroscience-based technology.

Sheila White is the Vice-President of Road 2 Eternity Media, a film and television production company, an administrator with Skyward Books. She is also a creative producer with Lightcore Animation and is the president of GO ON AND LIVE, a non-for-organization.

She is also a producer for JD3TV. Sheila enjoys empowering people through media, creating platforms, and enabling her clients to reach larger audiences to build a bigger, better, and stronger brand presence in the global marketplace both Nationally and Internationally.

Her professional team of experts provides family-friendly, faith-forward content that inspires, engages, motivates, encourages, and entertains audiences worldwide through print, film, audio, video, and animation.

Sheila White lives in the southwest suburbs of Chicago, IL, with her husband, three adult, successful children, and her niece. Sheila enjoys watching movies with her family and friends, eating healthy food, and cuddling with her Maltese puppy named Cody. You can learn more about her at https://www.road2eternity.net

www.ingramcontent.com/pod-product-compliance
Lightning Source LLC
Chambersburg PA
CBHW070815220526
45466CB00002E/672